NCEO

Thanks for Joining!

I wanted to add my personal thanks for becoming a member of the National Center for Employee Ownership. Don't hesitate to get in touch with me directly with any questions you might have.

I wanted to send along a complimentary copy of my book An Ownership Tale. I wrote this fable of a hypothetical company based on 30 years of actual experiences in real ESOP Companies. It's meant to be given out to company leaders, and/or employees more broadly. We priced it very close to our cost to make it easily accessible.

More details on the book are on our Web site at www.nceo.org. If you want to place a very large order, call me for special reduced pricing.

I hope you enjoy it, and, more generally, that you find membership in the NCEO worthwhile. I'd very much like to hear what you think about us and how we can serve you better.

Appreciatively,

Corey Rosen

Corey Rosen
Senior Staff Member and Cofounder

An

Ownership
Tale

Corey Rosen

An

Ownership

Tale

Corey Rosen

The National Center for Employee Ownership
Oakland, California

An Ownership Tale
Corey Rosen
Book design by Scott Rodrick

The National Center for Employee Ownership
1629 Telegraph Avenue, Suite 200
Oakland, CA 94612
(510) 208-1300
(510) 272-9510 (fax)
Web site: www.nceo.org

ISBN: 978-1-932924-52-7

Contents

Preface

The equation seems so simple. Give people a meaningful financial stake in their company, make sure they understand how it works, and watch the newly motivated employees help the company improve sales, quality, and profits.

Unfortunately, it is not that simple. The chance to accumulate a significant financial nest egg does motivate most people, but just being motivated at work is not enough to make a major difference in corporate performance. Working harder is important, but what really turns a company around is the presence of new ideas for doing the work better. It's the accumulation of small—and some not-so-small—ideas that employees can generate that improve efficiency and quality, increase output and customer satisfaction, save waste, reduce work-related injuries, and generate new product and service ideas that create an "ownership advantage" that competitors cannot copy.

Getting employees to contribute those ideas and put them into effect is not as easy as saying "now you are an owner, so go to it." Just having an open-door policy won't work either—few people will darken your doorstep. What is needed is a structure of participation. Employees must have specific ways to share their ideas, whether through team meetings, cross-functional teams, ad-hoc groups, staff meetings, or some other forum. These ideas need to be informed by good information. Employees need to know how to measure whether what they are doing will add to the bottom line. When this kind of employee involvement system is paired with the rewards of ownership, the results are impressive. ESOP companies with this "ownership culture" grow 8% to 11% faster than would have been predicted absent this combination.

This book is meant to help business leaders, consultants, ESOP committees, and employees understand how to create an ownership culture. The company and all the characters in the book except Jack Stack are fictitious, but the story is very real. It is based on 36 years of conversations with companies and employees about ownership culture. Everyone, every problem, every conversation, and every solution in the book is based on something I have seen many times.

BTA, the fictional company in the book, comes up with some fairly specific solutions to creating an ownership culture. You company will no doubt end up with some variation of the BTA approach. There is no specific road map to creating an ownership culture. The end result will always have some common feature—significant ownership for employees, good communications, sharing financial information, and a structure of employee involvement—but the specific end result will differ.

You can learn more about the many ways actual companies have created ownership cultures in our much more detailed book on this topic, *The Ownership Edge*. You can also learn more from our ownership culture webinar series, our annual *Get the Most Out of Your ESOP* meeting, or our annual conference.

Creating a happy ending to your own ownership tale will take a lot of work. It is well worth the effort, however. Just go to any ESOP conference and listen to the employee owners' stories about how their companies—and sometimes their lives—have been transformed and you will see why.

Acknowledgments

Several people provided terrific input for this book. Joe Cabral, former CEO of Chatsworth Products, an ESOP company, provided line-by-line editing and made very useful suggestions, especially about the manufacturing process and the financial statements. Loren Rodgers and Scott Rodrick of the NCEO staff gave detailed editorial assistance and advice.

Michael Quarrey, the director of operations at Web Industries (another ESOP company), a former NCEO staffer and a great friend, first suggested the idea for this book and was instrumental in its conceptual development.

Finally, a special thanks to Emma Lou Brent, former CEO of Phelps County Bank, whose leadership and commitment have set the standard for ESOP company CEOs.

2014 Reprint

In the time since this book was published in 2008, I have been gratified to see thousands of copies distributed, with the book becoming part of the ownership culture curriculum at many employee-owned companies. Unlike the legal and other technical matters affecting employee ownership, the principles presented here remain the same from year to year, so the text does not need updating in that sense. However, for the 2014 printing I have corrected a few typos; updated a few references to books, companies, and economic conditions; and inserted some additional text in the conclusion. Additionally, the book has been re-typeset.

Corey Rosen
October 2014

CHAPTER 1

In the Beginning

B ob Jacobson had just completed vesting in his company's employee stock ownership plan (ESOP). Like Bob, so had many people he worked with. The account values looked pretty good—a lot better than the retirement plans that most people would have had working somewhere else. Bob loved his job as CEO of Benson Thomas Associates (BTA), a company that had set up an ESOP five years ago and became 100% ESOP-owned through last year. But as good as the ESOP looked on paper, something was missing. Bob had read all the stories about how ESOPs turbo-charged company performance, how employee owners drove down costs and came up with all kinds of new ideas. He'd run into other ESOP company CEOs who just couldn't stop talking about their company's culture. But it wasn't happening at BTA. People just went about their jobs the way they always had. Not worse, not better. As Bob told his wife, Carol, "the ESOP is just kind of there—some people like it, some people are skeptical about it, most people just ignore it."

It wouldn't really matter that much, Bob supposed, if the company weren't facing some significant challenges. BTA was doing well, but the competition was getting tougher and the economy was not in the best shape. Bob really needed to get employees more engaged or some tough decisions would have to be made.

Frankly, Bob had no idea how to make that happen. What he did know was that it wouldn't just happen on its own. This is the tale of how Bob and BTA climbed up that hill. BTA does not really exist, but its story certainly does. While we made up Bob and everyone else in this tale, everything they learn and every misstep they take is based on real stories from real ESOP companies.

But before we can take that climb with Bob, we need to go back several years.

In the Beginning

The deal had looked great on paper. BTA's former owners, Mary Benson and Sam Thomas, had started the company in the early 1980s to provide innovative supply chain solutions for manufacturers. It had grown into a company that provided software to manage supplier relationships, warehouse services, and contract shipping. In the 1990s, it bought a company that manufactured storage systems and grew to 275 employees.

Mary was ready to retire by the late 1990s, but Sam wanted to stay on for a few years. He didn't have the money to buy her out. Selling the business was an option, but Sam really liked what he was doing and was not happy about the idea. A business associate, Alex Green, told him about the ESOP, a way the company could use tax-deductible dollars to buy Mary out and give Mary a tax deferral in the process.

"BTA would set up a trust, a kind of internal company safe deposit box designed to buy and hold shares for employees," Alex explained. "The trust would borrow money to buy Mary's shares. She'll get a tax benefit because she can defer paying taxes on the money she makes by reinvesting in other stocks and bonds. And the company could buy her out and take a tax deduction for the cost, something you can't normally do."

"That sounds like smoke and mirrors, Alex," Sam replied. "Just where does this money come from to buy the shares? The employees sure can't buy it."

"They don't have to," explained Alex. "The company would make tax-deductible contributions to the trust so it could repay the loan. So for every dollar that goes in, you can avoid about 40 cents in taxes. As the loan gets repaid, all full-time employees get allocations of stock in accounts set up for them."

"Over time, they become vested in these shares just as they would become vested in a pension plan. After they leave the company, the company buys the shares back from them. All the transactions would be based on what an outside expert determines to be a fair price," Alex continued. "Meanwhile, you could stay on to run the business."

"OK, so say we can really do this," Sam said. "But I am not ready to give up control to the employees. If they own the company, what if they want to fire me?"

Alex told him, "A trustee appointed by the board votes the ESOP shares, so you don't have to give up control unless you want to. Hey, you've got good profits this year and should for the foreseeable future. BTA can do this. It's a great solution."

After a few months of looking into this in more detail, Sam and Mary decided to proceed. They didn't tell the employees they were thinking about the ESOP, though. "It's really too risky," Sam said. "What if we don't end up doing it? This really is none of the employees' business right now. When the deal is done we can tell them." However, Mary thought telling them was the right thing to do. She worried the employees might think this meant the company did not trust them, but she went along with Sam.

When the ESOP was in place, Sam brought in John Evans, the lawyer who set up the plan, to explain it to people. "An ESOP is a qualified employee benefit plan that can use leverage to purchase shares. Shares are put into your accounts based on relative pay on each annual allocation date. Vesting occurs over several years. At termination, you will receive a distribution of your account balances." That's the gist of what he said, anyway. It actually took him 30 minutes and 27 PowerPoint slides. When it was over, he asked for questions. There weren't any, so Sam and Mary assumed people understood what was happening or at least understood enough to give it the benefit of the doubt. Right now they would just give employees the basics; they could always share more information later as the need arose.

Out on the floor, it was a different story.

"I don't have the vaguest ideas what he meant," Adam Stewart, a worker in the warehouse, told his wife that night, "and, frankly, neither did anyone else. People just had no clue what that lawyer was talking about. No one asked any questions because they didn't even know what to ask."

Rosario Chavez, a long-time employee who had become something of a confidante to Sam and Bob, heard from several people that the rumor was that Mary and Sam had had a falling out and that Sam was using this ESOP thing to buy Mary out, get some tax breaks, and, somehow, eventually take it out of employee paychecks. Adam had heard it, too. "But look," Rosario told him, "I've known Sam and Mary for years. They have been pretty good employers. You know, these cynics always somehow want to seem the smartest guys around—and lots of people seem to think they are, but I think we should give them a chance. I know the cynics somehow always seem smarter but maybe that's not true this time around."

Some Time Later...

And so it went for the first couple of years. Sam and Mary really did not do a lot to explain just what the ESOP was. "Look," Sam told Mary, "this is a good deal for these people. They pay zip for this stock. They're adults. We've given them the material, and, over time, they'll see what a good benefit this is. Spending a lot more time and money when people don't seem that interested now would be a waste of time."

Actually, employees were interested—just confused. "All we get is a piece of paper, some kind of annual statement. Beats me what it means or why I should care," Austin Everson told Rosario. "As far as I'm concerned, this is just funny money, pieces of paper. I don't see why they couldn't have just given us the money instead." Austin left after his third year, just before he would have had been in the plan and 20% vested.

Mary pushed Sam to do better. "At one of those ESOP meetings we went to," she told Sam, "I saw these nifty brochures from an ESOP company. We could use those to develop our own version. And maybe we can have a meeting once a year to actually explain to people how the statement works. The presenter from that company said he had meetings every year where he personally went over how the ESOP worked."

Sam grudgingly agreed. Mary took the brochures, made some changes so they described BTA, and had the company's printer lay out a new version they could pass around. Mary figured once people had the brochure they'd come and ask questions, but no one did. "I told you," Sam said. "It's just a waste of time and paper."

Adam, however, said the effort did net some results. "I think some people understood it better. There were still a lot of cynics, but fewer. Mostly the attitude became, 'Let's just wait and see if anything really comes of this,' like people actually getting paid for their shares." He didn't find it surprising that people didn't ask any questions. After all, most people wouldn't be getting anything out of the ESOP for a while.

But Sam was frustrated, and one day just blew up. "I remember he told me that he wished he had never set the ESOP up." Kevin Ellis, BTA's CFO recalled. "Sure," Sam said, "there were some nice tax benefits and it's a good deal for employees, but not once has someone come and thanked me for doing this. You know, we could have just sold the company—there were some offers. At the time I wanted to stay on. I like working here and, whether people believe it or not, I really did want to reward them for the years of hard work they put in. But I just don't see people acting like owners."

"I told him I don't think people really understood how the plan worked," Kevin countered. "We tell them we want them to act like owners, but I don't think they know what that means, much less what an ESOP is. Maybe we should spend some effort communicating this better. It's worth a shot."

"Fine," Sam shot back. "You think you can get these people to start paying attention with some whiz-bang communications program. So now it's your baby to rock. Just don't be surprised when I tell you I told you it wouldn't work."

Annoyed but determined, Kevin asked HR Director Karen Suzuki to develop a communications program. Karen was a gifted communicator, and people had come to like and trust her. She took on the program with enthusiasm. "I set up an orientation program for new employees where Kevin and I explained all the rules of the plan in the plainest language we could think of. Instead of waiting for questions, we asked employees to write down at least one question before coming. Their question entitled them to free pizza, and the question cards got entered into a drawing for gift certificates. Every six months we'd have a new program for recent hires and anyone who wanted a refresher course. We also added a plain-language employee handbook.

"Then we started an ESOP newsletter. There were frequently asked questions, columns about the company, brief explanations of one ESOP issue or another, and stories about what employees were doing outside of work. We got employees to contribute articles, too. We also put together a simple pamphlet explaining how the ESOP worked and gave that to everyone."

Kevin came up with the idea of adding features to the annual meeting. "I went over the company's progress in very general terms. I didn't want to give out specific financial information because I was worried it would get out to the wrong people. Anyway, I didn't think people would understand or even be much interested."

Sadly, a few years after the ESOP was started, Sam started having some heart problems. His doctor told him he needed to get away from the stresses of running the business and focus on getting well. BTA had done well enough to pay off the loan early. The chief operating officer, Bob Jacobson, showed promise as a potential CEO. The ESOP could buy out Sam and become 100% owner of the company. Even better, tax laws provided that as a 100% ESOP-owned S cor-

Sample text from the BTA *ESOP Handbook*

How Our Stock Value Is Set

BTA is not a company whose stock can be purchased on a stock exchange. So there are not people buying and selling it every day to create a market price. Instead, we have an outside expert come in every year to figure out what a buyer who had all the information needed would be willing to pay for BTA shares. Then the ESOP trustee looks at this report very carefully, asks a lot of questions, and decides if the appraiser has done a good job.

To understand what the appraiser does, say Jeff and Sally set up a business installing backyard ponds called Pond Builders. Over the next few years, they build up a good list of customers. They become well known in the business, and add on a training program for other companies and sell software on pool design and installation. Eventually, they decide to sell. There is some equipment, some used, some in pretty good shape. There are also the copyrights on the software, their customer lists, and some money clients owe them. These are all assets that could be sold to someone else. But the real value of Pond Builders is the company's ability to use these assets year after year to make profits. What a buyer really wants is the ability to have these profits to repay the cost of buying the business. Once that is repaid, the rest will be gravy.

So what the appraiser does is ask how much a buyer would pay to get control of these profits. The buyer will look at such things as:

• How risky is this investment compared to other investments I could make?

• If things don't work out, how much can I sell the assets for?

• How much are other people paying for companies like this?

• What's going to happen to the economy in general and the pool buying economy specifically?

The appraisal firm will use data from other companies, investment models, and its own experience to come up with a number, backed by a report that is usually 80 to 90 pages long. By using an experienced appraisal firm with a good reputation, we think we can have a value we can all believe is accurate.

A Few Questions Employees Asked

You make this plan sound like such a good deal to us. So what is in it for the owners?

If I am an owner, how come I can't vote my shares?

Will I get vesting credit for the years I worked before the ESOP started?

Can I get my money out of the ESOP before I leave?

What if the company goes bankrupt?

How can we know that the price we get for the shares is fair?

Will this affect our 401(k) plan?

How much money can I expect to be added to my account every year?

Who gets the shares left over if employees don't vest?

poration, there would be no federal income taxes due on any profit the company made. So the ESOP borrowed enough money to buy out Sam. He relocated to San Diego, started a new diet and exercise regime, and was feeling well enough now to get involved with his favorite charity, a national program to send underprivileged kids to summer camps. He was able to return to the company's board, but his new life kept him busy enough so that he didn't want to be any more involved.

So it all seemed to have worked out just great. The employees kept their jobs, Sam and Mary got cashed out, and the company was solid financially and now had this great tax break. ESOP account balances were well into five figures for much of the staff, at least those who had been there a while. People were starting to think maybe the ESOP really would be a nice benefit some day.

Bob sent out an email to everyone telling them that as owners, they could come talk to him any time with new ideas. "My door is always open," he said.

But something was missing, as Bob would soon find out.

CHAPTER 2

A Bump—Make That a Big Pothole—In the Road

Bob was having a very bad day. Kevin had just phoned him from Indianapolis telling him that BTA's biggest customer had just got a bid on supply chain management software from a company in India. "They like us, or so they keep saying," Kevin told Bob. "But, you know, they say 'business is business,' and unless BTA can match the Indian company's bid, they'll pull the contract. There's no way we can do that—you know that, Bob."

"Just what I need," Bob moaned. "I guess it was a sign when we lost that Hammond contract. It didn't seem like a big deal then, just like those three contracts we lost from some of the small accounts in warehousing because they said the housing market was no good and they had to cut back."

"It's not a crisis," Kevin reminded Bob. "We still have a solid cash position. We're still profitable enough, just less so."

"Maybe," Bob replied. "But what if we can't bid the software contract profitably? We're going to have to lay some people off unless we can find new clients, and the stock value probably will go down this year for the first time since the buyout—just when people are finally seeing a real benefit. The skeptics will have a field day."

Bob met with Kevin to discuss what steps to take. He asked Rosario to join them. He trusted her and thought she'd have a better sense for what people out on the floor were thinking. Rosario said they needed to tell people just what was going on. "They're the owners," said Rosario. "They deserve to know. More important, we really need them to know. Tell them it's time to really start acting and thinking like owners. Look for ways to cut costs and improve service. Don't spend time at work doing non-work things like shopping on the Internet or texting their friends."

Kevin was more skeptical. "What do we tell them? What's the story here? Some Indian company is going to eat them for lunch, frankly, because I just don't see how we can cut costs on that project enough to make it profitable. And the housing crisis is the housing crisis. They can't make that go away. I think we are just going to have to face the music and think about layoffs."

Bob was torn. "Kevin, they are the owners. You know what people say—they're owners in name only. Sure, the account balances look nice, but we do pretty much keep them in the dark."

"So what do you tell them?" Kevin said. "Give them the Knute Rockne speech to win one for the Gipper? So they go out and break their backs for us and we still lose the business? It will just make things worse."

"Kevin, give these people some credit. They're adults. If we just call them together one day and say, 'Guess what, 10% of you are getting laid off,' the 90% who remain will wonder if they're next. If we're upfront about it, at least they know what's coming—if it does—and maybe will believe us when we say we don't think it puts everything else at risk."

Kevin looked away in thinly disguised contempt. He always thought Rosario was too "squishy" about things. Bob's instincts sided more with Rosario, but he was afraid that Kevin might be more the realist. He said he'd think it over.

At Dinner That Night...

That night Bob decided to ask Carol about it. Carol was a level-headed woman with a very good feel for people problems. He didn't ask her business advice that much but tended to heed it when he did.

"Tell them, Bob. You've got people who've been there for years. They deserve to know what's going on and at least have a chance to do something about it. You take all this responsibility on your shoulders, but maybe some people might have some ideas you haven't thought about. Anyway, it is their company. Imagine you were in their shoes—what would you want your boss to do? Remember when you worked for Bill Irvin at GeoSupply and you were sure you knew how they could make save money on their invoicing system? And how frustrated you were that no one even gave you the chance?"

"I do," Bob said. "But that was different. I was a manager; I understood how business works. And I had options for other jobs. I think all we're going to do is scare people. Anyway I do welcome employee ideas. I ask for them over and over again."

"Give me a break, Bob. I know you're sincere about wanting their ideas, but you just have to realize it's hard for people. You can be intimidating, you know, even if you don't mean to be. Anyway if I were an employee I'd want to be told what was going on. Think about how you complain when airline pilots assume passengers shouldn't be told what's going on when the plane sits at the gate for 30 minutes. You'd rather know than just keep guessing, right? It seems like the same thing here."

"Yeah," Bob said. "Maybe you're right. I'll give it a shot."

So the next week Bob called a general meeting. Employees suspected something was up. Other than the annual ESOP meeting there weren't any gatherings like this.

"As you all know," Bob started, "since the ESOP, we've had a very good run. We've made money, we've added new people, we've been able to upgrade our facilities, and I think we've even had some fun in the process. But we are not immune to the same kinds of pressures other businesses face. Plastic Engineering is considering a bid from an Indian company. I don't need to tell you what that means. I understand their employees make a third as much as we pay. The housing slump has put some of our customers in a real crunch, and I expect less business from them in the coming year, at least. Direct Distribution is going to live up to its name and open up its own warehouses rather than contract with us.

"So we've got just a few choices. We can figure out ways to cut costs on the Plastic Engineering contract, but I won't kid you, we're probably talking about something pretty major. Kevin and I, along with Anna [Anna Sampson, the director of sales] are going to focus on looking for new business. Meanwhile, with the customers we still have—and that is most of them, remember—we need to find ways to be more efficient so that we make more money out of those contracts. In fact, if we just did that, we might be able to keep profits where they are.

"But I'll be honest. If we can't do these things, the only responsible thing is to lay some people off. If we don't, here's what happens. Profits go down, and we have less money to reinvest to keep the best technologies and equipment. So we become less competitive and maybe lose more business. That makes profits go down, and unless we find a way to break the cycle, we could find ourselves in a death spiral. I guarantee you that if we do lay people off, we'll treat those people well. They'll get a generous severance and all the help we can give them to find new jobs. But we have to be realistic.

"There is one more thing. We are all 100% owners of this company. If we really pull together and act as a team, we can get through this. I know you're giving 100% right now, but maybe we can all give 110%. We can learn to be more efficient, make sure other people don't slack off, share ideas on how things might be done better. I know we in management have not always been as open to your ideas as we should be, but from today on all of us are going to have an open-door policy. Don't hesitate to tell any of us just what you think we can do."

Employees stirred in their chairs. A few asked questions, but most just figured there was not much they could do but wait and see what happened. Some people decided to check out some online job listings just to see what might be out there.

CHAPTER 3

Open Doors, Empty Doorways

B ob went back to his office feeling pretty proud of himself. What he did was not easy for him. He'd spent years under Mary and Sam's tutelage. They had been generous but very traditional owners. Employees were paid well and got good benefits, but Sam and Mary made just about every decision that mattered, working long, long hours to do so. Bob had assumed he would take over their role in much the same way. After all, Sam and Mary hired him out of a competitor company because he was, they said, a decisive, smart, take-charge kind of guy. Bob had figured the ESOP would be just another benefit and that employees would be grateful for the chance both to own stock and keep their jobs.

But now that did not seem enough. For years, Bob, Kevin, and Rosario had been urging people to think and act like owners, but they never really thought through just how that would play out in day-to-day work. Now Bob thought he had really taken the leap. If employees wanted to act like owners, he had laid out just what they needed to do. And, for his part, he was genuinely ready to listen to their ideas. Carol was right. It really had made him angry when he worked for Bill Irvin at his old job, and it wasn't just how Bill had completely ignored what Bob thought was a very good idea on getting invoices paid faster. That was just the last straw, the one that made him slam the door angrily when he got home and rant for 20 minutes about the unfairness of it all.

He'd had other ideas, too. He'd go to talk to Bill about them, and Bill just patronized him. Or worse. Sometimes he would keep doing his email while Bob talked. Sometimes he would just say, "Thanks, Bob, I appreciate the input." Sometimes he asked for a memo —not more than one page, though. But not once did he follow through. It's part of why Bob left for BTA. He knew that one day he could run the show. So it was only fair to give the employee owners at BTA their chance to do what he always wished he could do with Bill.

So Bob called a meeting. "I've been thinking about us being employee owned," Bob told the employees. "And I've realized you have all the benefits of ownership, but, sometimes, it seemed like you have none of the obligations. It's not your own money. You don't have to make tough choices about the business. You don't have to pay attention to what's happening with our profits every day. But then I thought, 'Well, if they want to take more responsibility, how can they? When do they get the chance?'

"So starting today, any time someone has an idea about how we can make things better, they should talk to me personally. I promise to listen."

The next day Bob sent everyone an email with the same message. He bought a bunch of motivational brochures. There was the eagle soaring in the sky, tag-lined, "excellence is the result of caring more than others think is wise." A photo of rowers reminded them that teamwork is all about "pulling together," with nuggets from legendary football coach Vince Lombardi.

Almost no one actually walked in the door, no matter how many different ways Bob kept reminding people he really was being sincere. Adam did come in with an idea about rearranging the warehouse space to make it easier to track customers, but it was a bad time and Bob never did get back to him. And Thuy in accounting had a really good idea they actually put into place to get bills paid faster, but Kevin ended up taking most of the credit for it, saying he had been thinking about it all along anyway. Mostly, not much happened.

On her own Rosario had decided to go ask people what was up. She knew Bob really meant it (Kevin was not convinced about this "open door" thing, but she still thought he could come around if he saw some ideas work). So she set up a focus group. She asked

12 people from all areas to come talk to her about why Bob's open door just wasn't working. She wrote up a summary for Bob in the form of a dialogue but changed the names so people could speak more freely. Here's how it read:

Esther (software support): I do think Bob really means what he says, but we are really busting our tails right now trying to keep Plastics Engineering happy. Whatever they want, we do and more. Maybe if we are extra supportive they'll decide to keep us even if the price is higher. Anyway, there just isn't time to really sit down and think of new ways to do things.

Jimmy (programmer): Actually, I do have some ideas on how we could offer them a broader service than what they are getting now for the same price. But look, what I am supposed to do? Just walk away from my workstation to wait till Bob is off the phone or out of a meeting? How do I know my supervisor won't get mad and tell me I'm wasting time?

Sean (warehouse worker): There are a lot of things we do here just because we always did them that way. In my last job, they had some really cool systems we could use here too. They must cost something—I don't know. It's not my job to figure that out. So how do I know if it's worth it?

Enrique (warehouse worker): Look, say Kevin and I spent some time—even on our own—checking one of these things out. Like those scanner things that let you know where packages actually are all the time. And say it seemed OK to us. How do we know if it's worth the investment?

Sean (warehouse worker): Yeah, and even if we did, then what? I'm not exactly Mr. MBA. Am I supposed to go into Bob's office and lay out a spread sheet or what? I just don't think I have the skills to do this sort of thing. It's not what I got hired to do.

Kim (customer relations): Just about every day I hear some complaint or other. That's what I do, after all—try to smooth things over. So I hear all these problems, and tell people, you know, "We really do value your business and I promise we are going to work really hard to fix the problem. Meanwhile I'd be happy to offer a credit of 5% on your next purchase. Would that help?" I know enough to know that doesn't help us make a profit. What we need is to solve the problem. So I went to Bob and told him, and you know what he said? He said, "Kim, I appreciate that. What do you think we should do?" Like I would know what to do to fix a shipping delay. But, geez, if I can smell gas, shouldn't I tell someone even if I don't know how to turn it off?

Adam (warehouse): Actually, Kim, a group of us did get together on that problem after you told us. And we came up with a solution. So we went to Bob as a group; he listened patiently and really seemed impressed. He said he'd get back to us, but we're still waiting, and that was weeks ago.

Thuy (accounting): I guess that means I'm the only one who actually did have an idea that got accepted. I was really excited about it, too. No one ever listened before, and I felt great. "Empowered," as they say. But guess what? The next week Kevin tells me he had been thinking the same thing and wonders if maybe we hadn't talked about it some time. So don't ask me to do that again.

That Sinking Feeling...

Bob felt a little odd after reading the report. On the one hand, it was disappointing. In fact, the more he thought about it, the more depressing it was. "Am I the only adult in this company?" he wondered. "If I wasn't paying attention, would anyone take the responsibility to make sure things got done right? It sure feels like they would all sit around a table, not quite looking at each other, hoping that someone else would do something until the lights went out on all of them." Lost in the gloom and disappointment, Bob didn't notice

Thuy walk past his office several times looking inquisitively through the open door. The only plus side, he told himself, is that he could go back home and tell Carol, "I told you so."

"Look," he told her that night, "people just didn't seem to get it. No one is exactly beating a path through my open door. When I talk to employees about their being owners, a lot of eyes glazed over. Few people seem willing to make any more effort than they did before the ESOP. And when I gave people a quiz about the plan (he'd heard that it was a good way to remind people of how great the ESOP benefits were), it was clear almost no one really had a clue. Worse, there were some very loud cynics who kept telling people the ESOP was really a scam, that it would never really pay off. 'Just remember Enron and WorldCom,' they said, 'and what happened to people there.'"

"You're so impatient, Bob," Carol told him. "Give it some time—maybe get some advice from someone who has actually had an ESOP that worked. You don't have to reinvent the wheel, you know."

John Evans, the ESOP attorney, told him to be patient as well. "It can take years for people to really get it. When people start to leave with checks, it will mean a lot more. Meanwhile, maybe it would be a good idea to step up the communications program, get people to understand what this plan does for them better."

But Bob was so tired of the whole thing he seriously thought about taking another job or maybe looking for a buyer. Julie Simms, his plan administrator, however, told him he needed to give it another chance. "There are a lot of good resources out there," she said. "In fact, there's a seminar in Minneapolis next month on creating effective communications. I can get you a discount—why not give it a chance?"

Bob decided with all this investment, he'd give it one more shot. He and HR director Karen Suzuki went to Minnesota. There they met some people in the same boat—frustrated. But he also met company leaders who seemed positively evangelical about their ESOPs, and, even more impressive, non-management employees who talked about their company as if it were theirs. Bob and Karen came back charged up, with several ideas to try to communicate the plan better.

CHAPTER 4

Getting the Message Across

On the way back, Karen told Bob she learned eight key things from the meeting:

1. Focus on the things employees most want to know: How they get in the plan, whether there is any cost or risk, when they can get their money, and how it will be taxed.

2. People learn best when they actually get involved in using the information. That can be in quiz games about the ESOP, explaining the ESOP to other people, interactive Web sites, and employee-written newsletters. None of these things would be costly.

3. People learn better when they have fun. So there can be competition between teams to see which group knows ESOPs best. There can be food whenever there is an employee meeting. Maybe there can even be an ESOP skit.

4. Different people learn in different ways. Some like to read, some go to meetings, some use the Web, some listen to an audio tape. So using different approaches makes sense.

5. Stories are important. Newspaper articles on complex subjects always start with a personal story.

6. It's a good idea for employees to learn from one another. By creating an employee communications committee, employees could hear about the ESOP in their own language, and the committee members would themselves become more knowledgeable about the ESOP.

7. Repetition is good, so instead of trying to explain the ESOP all at once every year, it would be better to explain pieces of it on a regular basis. Break the ESOP content into smaller pieces and spread the content out over time: that way you can reinforce key lessons and gradually build up people's understanding without overwhelming them.

8. Explain how the former owners benefitted from selling to the ESOP. People want to know why this was done and are OK with the former owners getting a benefit, too. Being straightforward about this (and other issues, like the limitations on ESOP ownership and the financial risks of owning stock) makes the ESOP more credible.

Bob gave Karen the OK to move forward. So when they got back, she asked Adam, Thuy, Rosario, Enrique (who could help explain the plan to Spanish-speaking people), and Kim to join her on a new ESOP committee.

"This is just a first step," she told them. "If we can do this well, maybe we can move on to other things, too." They all agreed to give it a try.

There was a lot of enthusiasm at first. Their first big bash was the next month, and they ordered pizza for each shift and played "ESOP Jeopardy." Employees formed teams to guess the right questions to ESOP answers, like "six years" ("How long does it take our stock to vest?"). The winning teams received gift certificates on eBay.

Thuy volunteered to set up a frequently asked questions site on the Web site. She put up every question she had, then asked other people to submit their own. Bob and John Evans provided answers.

Adam took charge of creating a two-page monthly newsletter. Bob wrote a column on how business was going. Enrique contributed short snippets on things people were doing outside of work. Kim wrote a short piece on some aspect of the ESOP.

At the next gathering, Karen invited three employees and one former employee from a nearby ESOP company that had been doing well to come talk about their stories. Their plan was 18 years old, and they could talk about how some people had left with some pretty large accounts. When the former employee actually got her distribution, it was enough to get her three kids through college when they were old enough—the first kids in her family to do so.

One of the most unusual things they did was to ask people to create a video to show at another meeting. People were asked what they would do with their ESOP accounts one day if things went really well. It was fun to see the ideas people came up with. Esther planned to buy a house boat; Jimmy wanted to see every baseball stadium in the country. Of course, a lot of people just wanted to be able to retire without having to rely only on Social Security.

After several months, Karen sent out a survey to see how people were doing. "We are making progress," she reported to Bob. "Based on these data, about half the employees said they have a pretty good idea how the plan works. Another quarter say they have some idea but are confused about some things, mostly having to do with vesting. Another quarter still don't get it. We don't know exactly how that compares to six months ago, but based on that focus group, I'd say we've made some real progress." Bob agreed.

"But there's one piece that almost everyone is missing—valuation," Karen continued. "At first I thought it wasn't a big deal—that's such an arcane process that even I don't really understand it. But Thuy pointed out that valuation is really the key to everything: People need to know what drives changes in the stock price if they're going to have any impact on the value of their accounts. We don't need everyone to get an MBA, but we ought to make sure they understand what the valuation firm does with the profit numbers we give them."

So Bob asked Karen to fill in some of those gaps. The ESOP committee added a bit more information on valuation to the standard presentation and created a few posters on the topic. They set up a conference call with the person who did the valuation for BTA and learned the basics of valuation, including what factors employees can control and what they can't. They added more slides to the standard presentation and did a series of brown bag lunches about valuation. They figured out how much each employee would have to add to the bottom line in order to increase the value of the stock by five cents per share and wrote a newsletter article about cost-saving ideas.

Bob saw that as real progress. But as pleased as he was to see that people understood what was going on better, he didn't see much change in behavior. Oh, sure, people seemed a little more careful about waste or being nicer to customers. And some people were even putting in extra time or just spending less time at work chatting on their cell phones or buying clothes online. But this extra efficiency wasn't the kind of breakthrough that was needed. Plastics Engineering did cancel the contract. Kevin told Bob that unless they laid some people off, they'd lose money and the bank might want to talk about their loan. Anna Sampson had scared up some new accounts, but they would be profitable only if the company became a lot more efficient. Bob swallowed hard and decided to lay off 5% of the work force. He knew 10% would make more sense, but he just couldn't do it.

The members of the ESOP committee had been feeling good about themselves. The education program was good and getting better, and people were saving money for BTA and starting to sound like some of the other employees they had met at conferences. They each had a new credibility in the eyes of other employees, and they were proud. When Bob asked for their help in telling everyone the news about the layoffs, they were shocked.

After a few minutes of silence, Adam said, "Well, I feel pretty stupid now. I know you showed us a lot of numbers and talked about the risk of stock and all that, but I had no idea that the numbers we were seeing meant that layoffs were coming. How could I know that? I don't know when 'bad news' means layoffs and when it just means you just want me to work harder. I had nothing to do with this decision, I don't like it, and I'm not going to cover for you on this one. The employees are doing their part. I guess you didn't do yours." He got up to leave.

Bob said, "Adam, please. Hold on for just a minute. Look, I have lost sleep over this. I know, I know, I'm not the one being laid off, and it probably seems insulting to say, 'I feel your pain.' But trust me, this is the hardest thing I have ever had to do.

"I suppose it would have been better if I had shared the bad news all along with everyone so these things wouldn't come as a big surprise. But I worried that if I did people would get scared. And maybe we could find a way to work around the problems anyway. But I didn't, and I take the blame for that. I also learned a lesson that I need to be more open with you. After all, you're the owners."

Karen had been thinking about these issues, too. She usually was a bit timid about challenging Bob, but she decided now was the time to speak up: "Bob, I believe you. I really do. But talk is not enough. If we're really going to learn from this, we need to develop a contingency plan for the next time. Let's come up with a plan for what to do when business turns down. Is the first resort to lay people off? Maybe we can do voluntarily unpaid leave, or people can decide it's better for us all to shorten our work hours. Let's make layoffs the last resort, not the first. Because, I'll tell you, it's not just the 5% getting laid off you need to worry about. It's the 95% who remain who worry they'll be next."

A few people stood up and applauded. Soon everyone was on their feet. Bob agreed he'd meet with Karen to draft a plan and then run it by the ESOP committee. He'd get back to people in the next two weeks.

The contingency plan was a good start. But it didn't solve the problem of becoming more productive. To get there, things needed to change.

CHAPTER 5

Leaps of Faith

At the Minnesota meeting, Bob had met Maggie Brooks, the ex-CEO of a successful 100% ESOP-owned wholesaler in a small town in Iowa. She was rhapsodic about what the ESOP had done for them. Two big national competitors had moved into their market over the last several years, but her company had actually gained market share and grown profits. "Our people really saw it as a challenge," Maggie said. "They were not about to be pushed around by the big guys. People just put their heads together and came up with dozens of ideas, big and small, to provide better service in a more profitable way. And they just keep doing it. You'd be amazed at all the ideas they have. It was just so much fun to go to work with people that engaged. Our stock has grown 17% per year since the ESOP, and we have a janitor with 20 years of service with $300,000 in his account."

Bob had gotten her card and decided to give her a call. Maggie suggested Bob come to visit the company and spend a day talking to her and employees. Bob booked a flight for the next week.

"I was just blown away by your story, Maggie. But we've done a lot of the same things you have and have not had the same results. We're a similar size and have somewhat similar businesses. We're both 100% ESOP. Like you, we've done a lot to educate people about the plan. And hardly a day goes by when I don't ask people for ideas. But not much has really changed. Maybe you're just lucky—you've got the right people in the right place. Frankly, our people don't seem to care as much as they should."

"About 15 years ago, Bob," Maggie said, "I was pretty much where you were. The ESOP wasn't my idea—frankly, the owner just wanted the tax benefits. In fact, he didn't like the idea of 'giving' people shares. He would have rather they had to pay for them, like he did. But ESOPs don't work that way, and he wanted to retire. He also was pretty skeptical about employees acting like owners. That just wasn't their place, he thought. You hire managers to run the company, after all.

"When he left, we did what you did. We did a lot of communications about the plan, telling people what a good deal this was for them and how much money they could accumulate over time. And we did a pretty good job, too. But not much really changed.

"So I called the National Center for Employee Ownership and asked them what else we could do. I'd seen in their newsletter research that ESOPs really improved corporate performance in most companies, so I wanted to see what the secret was.

"Their director came out and spent the day here. He told me the secret was pretty simple to explain, but also pretty hard to do. He said we had a good start with our communications and our plan was rich enough to get people's attention. But it was not enough just to ask people to get involved; you had to set up specific structures. The one thing that really struck me about what he said, in fact, was that 'Participation doesn't happen because you allow it; it happens because you structure it.'

"I think I had a good relationship with my employees. That's what our surveys said, anyway. In fact, we applied for, and won, a couple of local 'best place to work' awards. People said they like their jobs and the company. But people can be satisfied with work for lots of reasons—good pay, good friends at work, a job they find interesting and challenging, opportunities for job advancement, fun social events, and supportive supervisors, for instance. But there is a difference between being happy with your job and being fully engaged in contributing ideas and information. I guess I always figured that if we scored so well on worker satisfaction that meant people would be engaged, but it wasn't happening.

"I could see just encouraging participation is too ambiguous. People don't know how or when to share ideas, how much authority they have to make decisions, when suggesting an idea will seem like stepping on someone's toes, or how to evaluate their own ideas to see if they make any sense. There also isn't any kind of stimulation to get people thinking about problems, as there would be in a meeting to address an issue. So no one does anything.

"We needed structures to get people into situations where they are expected to come up with ideas and have a forum where they can actually do something about them. So what we did to start was set up an 'Employee Problem Solving Process.' It was simple and easy to get going. First, we created a steering committee made up of managers and employees who volunteered for it. They met a few times and came up with the program.

"What they did was to create a 'Problem Form.' The form asked people to identify anything they saw that was making it harder to serve customers better, operate more efficiently, create new services, etc. Anything was fair game. You didn't have to have a solution to the problem, but if you did have an idea, it was welcome.

"The form asked people to describe the problem and give an example or two. It asked for some specifics, if people knew them, such as how often it happened, how much it was costing, and what the source of the difficulty was. Then it asked people whether they had any ideas to solve it, with space for outlining costs, time involved, who might work on it, and any other issues they wanted to raise. People only had to fill in what they could.

"The forms were sent to the committee every week for review. Some were 'no brainers,' simple things that could be fixed right away. For instance, one problem we were having was that people did not always know that certain shipments needed priority. So we created a more flexible process for determining shipment dates. Others were more in the nature of gripes than real business issues. Most required some processing, though. In some cases the committee

The BTA Problem Form

Name _____

Date _____

Describe the problem in the space below:

What kinds of problems does not resolving this issue create? Use the issues below as a guide and be as specific as possible:

> Poor quality
> Unhappy customers
> Wasted time
> Extra costs
> Missed opportunities
> Environmental issues, including excess energy use
> Morale problems
> Other

How often does the problem come up?

Have you tried to resolve this problem before? If so, describe what happened.

Do you have any suggestions on how to resolve it? Be as specific as you can, addressing (if possible) what materials, time, information, changes in work organization, or other issues that need to be addressed.

Sign and date below

REPLY FROM THE COMMITTEE

EMPLOYEE TO SIGN OFF IF SATISIFED WITH RESPONSE

If you are not satisfied, please provide an explanation for further review.

would set up an ad-hoc group, describe the problem, appoint a few people they thought needed to be on the committee, and then ask anyone else who wanted to volunteer to join it. The ad-hoc group met until it came up with a recommendation. The steering committee then reviewed it. Some ideas got sent back for more work. If the idea had merit, however, the committee could assign a group of people to implement it or, if the cost and time were significant or management otherwise needed to be involved, they would get the relevant management people together to come to a decision.

"Whatever they did, the resolution was sent back to the person proposing it who had to sign off on it before it could be considered closed. All the accepted ideas were posted on our internal Web site and in our monthly newsletter.

"The system worked—well, it worked pretty well. We were getting an awful lot of ideas, but people didn't seem to have a real good understanding of whether the solutions were worth the cost. I realized that you couldn't really blame them. They just didn't have the information to figure that out. We started sharing more numbers in a monthly meeting—the overall financials, then the key measurements for each area of work, things like on-time shipping scores, customer satisfaction, efficiency of warehouse space use, and packaging costs. We had our CFO do some analyses to see how improving these different numbers would affect the bottom line, and then we shared that with everyone on a regular basis.

"It wasn't always a cakewalk. At first, a lot of trivial ideas got raised, along with some really bad ones and just plain grousing. We wasted a lot of time. But we also used these as opportunities to teach people how to come up with better ideas the next time. It was a *lot* of work, and there were times I wanted to just can the whole thing. But we also got a few really good ideas, and that seemed to make it all worthwhile. After a year or two the ideas got better and better, with fewer misses and more hits."

Bob was impressed but daunted. Where to start? Should they just implement Maggie's plan? She urged him not to. "It worked for us, Bob, but each company is different. You need to find your own way. Here's what I suggest. First, don't do what we did and start solving problems before you have a system in place for people to understand the impact of what they are doing on the bottom line. Next month, there's a great conference in St. Louis called 'The Gathering of the Games.' It's about the Great Game of Business, probably the best worked-out system for sharing numbers. You'll get a lot of good ideas. Bring a few people with you. Then get your steering committee—you're going to start one, right, Bob?—to read some books on ways to get people involved, like *The Great Game of Business* or *Ideas Are Free.* Send a few people to a conference that covers these ideas. Go visit a few companies that have a lot of employee involvement. You're taking on a major effort here, and you should spend the time and resources to do it right, the same as you would to make any other major and costly business decision."

CHAPTER 6

The Numbers Game

Kevin Ellis, the CFO, was still skeptical. "Maybe it worked for Maggie," Kevin said, "but you know our people. They want to do their jobs and go home. They don't want to have to become finance experts. And if we give them information, who knows what they'll do with it or whether they can use it right. It seems to me that there's plenty of downside without much benefit."

Bob knew Kevin needed to be on board on this. Either he had to be convinced, or he needed to be replaced. So Bob sent Kevin, Anna Samson (the sales director), and Karen Suzuki from HR to the Great Game conference. "Just go, Kevin. At the very worst, you'll have a couple of days in a nice hotel. Listen to what your peers say and tell them about your concerns."

Kevin agreed—he always wanted to see the Gateway Arch in St. Louis, where the conference was—and he was a big Cardinals baseball fan. On the first day, they learned about SRC Holdings, the company that started this all.

Back in 1983, Jack Stack was the manager for a dying division, then called Springfield ReManufacturing, of what was then International Harvester (now called Navistar). It employed 139 people, but the prospects for keeping the company going seemed bleak. The remanufacturer of diesel engines was losing money, and so was the parent. Stack knew the plant would be closed soon unless somehow the employees could buy it.

He was enthusiastic about the idea but not naïve. He knew it was a long shot to get International Harvester to agree as well as to get financing. But his experience as a manager also convinced him that they could be a lot more productive than they were, productive enough to make money. The key was to get people a lot more engaged, to get them focused on how the operation made money. He had an innate trust for people. He didn't believe he had all or even most of the answers, but he was sure the person running the machine or ordering inventory had a lot of ideas about how things could be done better.

So he brought together a group of managers and proposed that they and an ESOP buy the company. Management used some of its own money to buy shares; the ESOP got the rest.

Stack approached International Harvester. The people in charge of figuring out what do with the plan were skeptical that employees could buy it, but they didn't exactly have a lot of people with better proposals. The managers at the plant all wanted to give the idea a go and were willing to put up their own money to help make it happen. Now Stack just had to borrow millions of dollars more. In fact, the loan they needed would be 89 times bigger than the equity managers were putting down. Deals like that just don't get done, but after 49 bankers told them no, the 50th banker said yes.

The impact of the debt was that Springfield could not lose $10,000 in a month and stay solvent. So Stack started a process to make sure everyone knew exactly what that meant. Considerable time was spent teaching all the employees, most of whom had high school educations, how to read a financial statement. The numbers were posted regularly to track progress. Every week managers and supervisors held a "huddle" to project all their relevant numbers in some detail. Variances from targets were analyzed, and new numbers set. This group then went out to the floor and huddled with the employees to go over the overall numbers and their own group's numbers, providing an opportunity to discuss ideas for improvement.

The overall financial numbers were important but not very immediate to people. So Stack and his colleagues started figuring out "critical numbers." These were the few things that kept managers up at night. Some were targets that had to be achieved; others were weaknesses that had to be addressed. There were corporate numbers as well as local numbers. Cash flow was the initial key critical number at the corporate level, for instance. But local groups could have something very different. It might be the amount of time it took to rebuild an engine or how long inventory stayed in stock. Groups came up with "mini-games" to identify their critical numbers, set a goal over a few months, and then get rewards if the goal was achieved, usually something fun.

The system was a remarkable success. Stack wrote a book about it called *The Great Game of Business* that became a business bestseller. People came from all over the world to see how they were doing it. By 2014, the stock, once worth 10 cents, was worth over $390, and the company, now named SRC Holdings to reflect its multiple divisions, employed 1,400 people with more than 13 lines of business, almost all of them created out of employee ideas.

Stack's mantra was that financial numbers are really not that complicated if you spend the time teaching people. They are no more complicated, for instance, than sports statistics. Knowing the numbers helps people make good decisions, but it also is very motivating. Business is a great game, he says. Knowing the score and all the statistics that go along with it makes playing the game a whole lot more fun.

The conference brought people together from dozens of companies who had their own takes on the process. A music company that was a developer and seller of children's music instructional programs, held meetings for all staff every single day. Every individual had numbers to track and report on. There were group and company numbers, too. The short meetings were held standing up in rapid-fire fashion, processing lots of information and ideas every day. People went through extensive training to learn the numbers as part of their orientation.

Lots of companies, such as SRC, have reached a point where budget numbers no longer came from the top down but from the bottom up. Employees in groups now devised their own critical numbers and set their own rewards. A food retailer, for instance, has teams in each department of each store that do this, posting their numbers for everyone to see. Companies created all kinds of scoreboards to track numbers, some literally with flashing lights. Some companies brought in community college people to teach finance; others sent people from all levels to industry training programs to learn the business better. One company they heard from, a small engineering company with an ESOP, stopped having the CFO present financials and rotated the task to a different employee each time. That way people really had to learn the numbers and how they worked.

Kevin came prepared to be skeptical, but as a numbers guy himself, the results these companies were achieving were pretty impressive. Even more impressive was the fact that a lot of the presenters were line employees in polo shirts or company T-shirts, people just like BTA's employees. They were enthusiastic and remarkably knowledgeable. Kevin was ready to give it a try, although he told Karen and Anna he still wondered if it really would work for them. "Maybe they just sent their stars," he said.

Anna and Karen were not so qualified in their enthusiasm, however. They picked up several good ideas and were eager to take them back.

Back at BTA, the three of them reported on their impressions of the conference and what ideas they wanted to implement at BTA. Bob listened to their story and assigned the three of them to form a committee to come up with a starting effort. They decided the next month to present a simplified income statement and balance sheet but not give people anything in writing, just a visual presentation and discussion. Then they would divide the employees into groups and figure out one key thing that that group could do to make the company perform better. The three of them would come up with the numbers first, but then a few months later they'd ask the employees to come up with their own. If they hit the targets, everyone on the team would get free dinner and movie tickets for two.

CHAPTER 7

From Open Doors to Open Book

I t took a few months to roll out the numbers, and there were a lot of bumps along the way. "We see the income statement," Sean in warehouse told Enrique. "But that's just one set of books, the one we see, not the ones that Kevin gives Bob." "One set, two sets, three sets—it's all just boring, complex stuff. Who can read this stuff?" Enrique shot back. "I would actually like to know how we are doing," Kim from customer relations added, "but these terms just don't mean much to me."

So after the first go-round, Karen tried a radical idea. She called in Thuy, Rosario, and Jimmy, all of whom had expressed some initial interest in the numbers, and told them "I want you to figure out a better way and to make the next presentation. Do it on work time, and Bob said we'll compensate you with some gift certificates too."

At their next meeting, Karen told Kevin and Bob about the task force. Kevin was still appalled. "You can't be serious. Who knows what they'll tell them?" But Karen was determined. She told Bob, "Kevin's level of knowledge is on a different planet compared to the work force. These people can speak the employees' language. And if they have to explain it, they'll learn it themselves really well. Remember, that was one of the key lessons of communicating."

Bob settled on a compromise. The three employees would make the presentation, but Kevin could be there to gently make any corrections. "Remember, Kevin, Thuy will be there. She's got some experience with this. Let's give it a shot," Bob told him.

Rosario said the team need a name, so they brainstormed a while. There was "Numbers R Us," "CSI BTA—Cost Science Investigators," "Spilling the Books," and more, and they ultimately settled on "The Numbers Team." Jimmy came up with a Web site to put up the numbers with hyperlinks to define each term. Thuy translated the accounting language into simple concepts. "Depreciation" became "wear and tear on things we bought," accounts receivable became "money customers owe us," and cash flow became "cash in minus cash out." Rosario created a comparison of all these numbers to someone's personal income and assets. The simplified income statement ended up looking like the one on the next page.

They used a similar simplified approach to create a cash flow statement and a balance sheet. Because of a large capital expense that year, cash flow actually was somewhat negative. They also created some colorful charts and graphs that compared their critical numbers from year to year. These included sales, profits, backlog, customer complaints, and order turnaround time.

They ran the presentation by Kevin, who reluctantly admitted they did a pretty good job. Then they met with the employees to try it out. This time they divided everyone into tables, and when the talk was over they asked each table to discuss the numbers and come up with two or three questions. That way, no one had to feel silly about asking something, since it was the group's questions.

Table one wanted to know how the company could end up with less cash in reserve at the end of the year than the year before but have more profit. "It's that second set of books," Enrique whispered to his tablemate Jesse.

"It's depreciation—wear and tear," Thuy explained. "See, when we buy something like those new shrink wrappers, we have to spend a lot of cash all at once. But we can use it over several years, so we charge part of the cost each year. The depreciation shows up over several years on the income statement, but the outlay of cash occurs immediately. So the cash statement looks like we lost money but the income statement looks like we made money."

A Simplified Income Statement

	What It Means	Two Years Ago	Last Year	Current Year	Budget
Sales	The total amount we billed for the year	$7,200,000	$7,800,000	$7,900,000	$8,400,000
Cost of goods sold	How much we paid for the things that go into our sold products, like labor, raw materials, rent, utilities, etc.	$6,400,000	$6,900,000	$7,200,000	$7,500,000
GROSS PROFIT	Sales minus the cost of goods sold	$800,000	$900,000	$700,000	$900,000
Selling, general, and administrative expenses; includes depreciation (annual wear and tear) on assets used in business	Costs other than the costs of goods sold, like sales and administrative salaries, office supplies, advertising, travel, etc.	$320,000	$310,000	$290,000	$320,000
OPERATING PROFIT	Gross profits minus sales, general, and administrative	$480,000	$590,000	$410,000	$580,000
Interest		$200,000	$220,000	$245,000	$250,000
ESOP contribution	Cash or shares contributed to the ESOP	$100,000	$100,000	$100,000	$100,000
EARNINGS BEFORE TAX		$280,000	$370,000	$255,000	$330,000
Income tax* or state taxes		0	0	0	0
PROFIT		$180,000	$270,000	$155,000	$230,000

*Because BTA is 100% owned by the ESOP, there is no income tax. If we were not a 100% S corporation ESOP, the owners would pay about 35% or so in taxes, which the company would fund with distributions. There are no state taxes in our state for S corporation owners.

"Seems what you're really doing is just pretending we have money we don't have," Adam said. "If I have less cash at the end of the year, I figure I lost money."

"Well," Thuy said, "let's say we didn't do it this way. We have a profit sharing plan here. So this big expense would come out of your profit share. Say you left next year, then the people who came next would get the benefit because the profit would look bigger—but you paid for it!"

"I guess that makes sense," Adam replied.

Table two wanted to know why if the profit was holding pretty steady, the stock price actually went down by 8%. Julie said, "You keep telling us if the profit goes up then the share price will go up. So, like, what gives with this?"

"In the long term it will go up, but other things matter in the short run, too, like what happens to stock in general," Thuy said. "Remember what our appraiser told us—the fair market value of our company is what a willing buyer would pay us. If buyers think that stocks are not a good investment in general, maybe because there are some really good interest rates around, they'll pay less for any company, including ours. Or if they think our industry won't do well in the future that would make them pay less, too. It's like making home improvements. In the long run, it will make your house worth more, but in a bad housing market and tough economy, your house price might go down even though you remodeled the kitchen. But it would have gone down even more if we didn't—and our stock price would be even lower if we didn't make a profit.

Table three wanted to know about executive pay. "We work our tails off in sales," Anna said. "And you say that the more profit we make, the more our stock is worth. But how do we know executives aren't just using the profit to pay themselves more?" Lots of employees looked furtively at Kevin to see what shade of red he was turning.

"We had a chance to talk about that with the appraiser," Rosario said. "She needs that information because if the company pays its executive too much she has to refigure the numbers on profit as if they were paid a wage more like the market would. She told us that the pay was reasonable. The board of directors looked at what people make in other companies with similar jobs, and they looked at whether the top people here are meeting their performance targets. She told us that the pay was very fair and that if we paid less, we could lose these people."

"So why not just tell us how much they make?" Anna asked.

Kevin couldn't help himself. "Look, would you want everyone to know how much you make? We really are very conservative about pay. But at the end of the day you'll have to trust us, because we just don't feel comfortable right now discussing it more."

Jimmy quickly moved on to table four, which had a question about how much they paid for computer services. Despite the awkwardness about the pay question, Kevin had to admit people were asking good, relevant questions. And they showed a lot more interest than he had ever expected.

Even Sean had to admit the new process was clearer. "I appreciate all the work these guys did. I still don't know what to do with all this information, but it was good to see it." Enrique was enthused: "I really feel like the company is making an effort, and we should give them a shot."

From the Big Picture to the Small Screen...

"This is all very interesting," Karen said, "but what exactly can we do with these big-picture numbers? Not much."

"Well," Thuy said, "we need to 'drill this down,' as they say, to things people can do something about. In *The Great Game of Business* we learned about 'mini-games' that let us tackle smaller issues people can get their hands around."

With help from Kevin and Bob, the numbers team came up with three critical numbers to work on: increasing on-time shipments by 10%, reducing overall costs by 2%, and increasing profits for the next quarter by 1%. They seemed like modest and achievable goals.

Everyone got the numbers. Each week Thuy put up a big chart in each work area showing progress. If the targets were met, each employee could be in a raffle pick from a list of local restaurants and get two movie tickets.

Three months passed, but only the profit goal was met. "I told you," said Sean. Esther told her husband they wouldn't get that dinner. He wasn't surprised. "I think they just picked a number that you couldn't meet. It's a sham." Julie wanted to give Bob and Karen some slack, but she wondered whether this new concept would get shot down by its initial failure.

CHAPTER 8

Making Progress

There were still a lot of skeptics, but Jimmy was determined to see this new open-book system through. As he saw it, the problem was twofold. First, the employees had no input into the numbers. "The plan was to let us pick numbers the second time around, but we should have done it from the start. If those were our goals, we'd have tried a lot harder to meet them. Maybe Kevin, Bob, and Karen can just provide us feedback, but we need a role in picking these numbers. Plus, we had no real way to figure out what to do. I guess the idea was just to work harder and more carefully, like turning off the lights when not in use and putting in an extra few minutes each day. But that's nickel and dime stuff. Esther and I, for instance, had an idea to create a program to let warehouse people track shipments more easily, but it would have cost a few thousand bucks, and we didn't have any way to make it happen."

Anna Sampson, the sales director, had been an early supporter of the effort, but she was pretty disappointed, too. "The goal of cutting costs was too vague. I can cut sales costs by not traveling as much, but is that really good for the business? Won't that undermine the profit goal?" Enrique from warehouse said, "We all know how we can get stuff out the door faster—don't double-check it to make sure it's right."

Kevin felt vindicated. Bob felt discouraged, and Karen wondered if all this effort would be wasted. Bob decided to call Maggie and ask what she thought.

"Look, Bob, who said this was going to be easy? You're trying to change the culture there. Don't expect it will change overnight, or even in the first several months. And certainly don't expect the first thing you try will work. It would have just been luck if it did. Take a look at what happened. Talk to the employees. Try to improve the process. Give it two or three more tries before you give up, but I'll bet one of those will work."

So Bob told Kevin and Karen to try again. This time Karen invited the skeptics like Sean and Esther to help design a new program. "If they own it, maybe they'll push harder instead of telling people it's all a waste of time," she told Bob. But she made sure people like Jimmy were there, too, people with some specific ideas on how to improve things.

The team decided to go to each working group and have members come up with their own critical number, anything that they thought would add to the bottom line. Then the numbers were reviewed by Kevin and Bob, who also were asked to come up with a company-wide goal. If a group met its goal, there would be a reward of the members' own choosing worth up to $50 per employee. If the company-wide goal were met, there would be a bonus of 2% of pay. Each group would come up with its own team name, post its progress for everyone to see and invite people to their meetings from other areas if they had ideas. Jimmy set up a section on the Web site where the numbers could be posted as well and people could make suggestions.

This time there was real progress. The "Boxing Team" in warehouse decided it needed to come up with a way to cut back on shipping errors. As in most companies, warehouse workers were boxing small stuff in dozens. That's just the way everyone did it. But too many customers were calling to say they were one short, while employees were also looking at inventory and finding out sometimes they put too much in the box.

The team looked at a lot of ideas. "We could just figure out how much each item weighs, put them on a scale, and not have to count them," Jorge suggested. Jack said they could buy boxes specific to each product so that by filling the box they would automatically know it was right. "Quick," said team member Mohammed. "What is 27 dozen? How about 27 10s? Easy, right? So why not ship by 10s?"

In the end, they settled on 10s. After three months, there was a 10% improvement, beating their goal, and they all got tickets to the ball game.

Team "Pay Me Now or Pay Me More Later" had a goal of reducing accounts receivable waiting time. Sally suggested increasing the penalty for late payment, but Bill said he got enough flak from customers about the 5% per month they already charged. "They just complain, go around us to sales or Kevin, and get an excuse."

"Why not just hand it over to an agency?" Barbara suggested.

"Do you have any idea what they charge?" Karen replied.

"Yeah," Bill said, "and just what we need, customers even more annoyed than they already are about our nagging."

"So what's your great idea, Einstein?" Barbara said, not entirely in jest. "How about if we take the opposite approach?" Karen replied. "We could send them a funny card—I don't know, maybe something like 'the dog ate my payment'—and say we hadn't gotten theirs yet, either. It would get their attention—it's different—and build some good will. Then if that fails, we can ramp things up a bit and be tougher."

The group decided to give it a try. It did make some improvement, but not quite enough to meet their goal. But they got good feedback from customers and thought with some tweaking it could work.

The software group team, "Eek It's a Geek," wrote a program analyzing energy usage and proposed a way to reduce it by 10%. Esther, the resident vegetarian, bicycle-commuting greenie, was leading the charge. "Look," she said, "these peripherals are vampires when we leave them on overnight. Let's get some of those power strips that cut off power to peripherals when the computer they're attached to is turned off. And we can put in sensors to turn lights on and off in rooms when people walk in. We can replace all the light bulbs with energy-efficient ones."

John said the programmers could work on developing software that drivers could use to plot the most energy-efficient routes: "I heard that UPS actually plans routes for all right turns because it saves gas and turns out to be faster overall. Little things like that add up."

Evan said they should have an energy audit by an outside company to look at insulation, solar panels, on-demand water heaters, etc.

Not all the ideas turned out to be worthwhile, but energy use did drop, and there was a side benefit that people were taking pride in the fact that their company was greener.

Even Kevin had to admit he was impressed. "I don't want to tell you I told you," Bob said, "but, well, I did. Sure, these ideas are not going to all of a sudden solve every problem. But they show that if we give people the chance and the *structure*, they can make a difference."

Rosario felt vindicated: "Hey, this first step worked pretty well. So step two is to make employee involvement part of the culture here. I've been talking to some other ESOP companies, and they gave me some good ideas about things we can do. There were a bunch of them, like forming teams in each work area, setting up cross-functional committees on things like safety, and setting up a Web site where people can discuss ideas."

Bob, feeling very good about the change he now saw as an idea he initiated, gave an eager thumbs up.

And the Forecast Is...

The mini-games were a good start, but only that. They got people used to working together on manageable problems, but the games, by definition, were meant to solve specific issues. After the first round of success it got harder to find more games on an ongoing basis. They were more of an ad-hoc approach that made a lot of sense from time to time but not a way to use the management of numbers to permeate the system.

Thuy said that as she understood Stack's Great Game model, the key was forecasting. Managers, supervisors, and employees all had to get together regularly to forecast their important numbers, whether sales, backlog, inventory turnover, the time it took for bills to be paid, or any number of production data, such as units produced per hour worked, number of shipments per day, and so on.

The committee wanted to roll the program out to everyone all at once, but Kevin would have none of it. "Even most of our managers have no experience with this," he told Thuy. "To expect supervisors and line employees to do this is just too much." Thuy and the rest of the committee agreed to start with managers, but only with the promise that if it worked, they would move down to supervisors, who at least would report their numbers to employees.

Before the first meeting, Bob told the 12 managers to come to the meeting with projections for next month's sales, backlog, profits, cash flow, productivity, and shipments/returns. Each manager made forecasts for his or her area. Most were pretty conservative. As software manager Josh Parsons told Kevin later, it made sense to low-ball the numbers so his group would look good the next time.

But after a few months of this, problems were coming up. "We keep beating our forecast," Bob said, "and that seems great, but, frankly, to me it just seems we aren't very good at forecasts."

With the 12 managers sitting around the table, Bob invited Anna Sampson and Warehouse Supervisor Adam Scott to explain why. "So Josh, you predicted that we would ship 240 units of the new software program," Adam said. "I used those numbers to draw up the schedule. It turns out that we actually sold 320, so I had to add overtime to get them out the door. If I had a better projection, I could have moved people off some other lower-priority jobs." Anna told logistics manager Rolf Hermann that his projection of being able to get by with the existing number of trucks for the next three months made it difficult for her to finalize a sale with a customer who needed short-term shipping support for the next three months—"a new customer who, with a good experience, might become a permanent one."

"That's easy for you to say, Anna. But what if you didn't get that sale? How was I supposed to know if was going to happen? My job is to minimize shipping costs, not keep unnecessary trucks for who knows what."

"So what should I do?" Anna snapped. "Not make the sale? Hey, I need to have your support if I am going to go out there and create markets."

The same pattern emerged in other areas as well. By the end of the meeting lots of nerves were frayed. "What this shows," Bob lectured, "is that you people actually need to talk to one another. I've asked you to do it over and over. But no, you're too busy, or you don't think the other person gives a damn. Next time, talk to one another, people, and be more accurate."

"I told you that was a dumb idea," Kevin said. Bob, however, was not at all unhappy. "I think it was actually pretty great, Kevin. This may be just what we need to get people to work better together. I've tried imploring them till I am blue in the face. The numbers make it real."

The next round went better, although some people still had trouble figuring out how to do this. Six months later Karen told Bob she heard Anna inviting Rolf onto a customer call to explain the advantages and disadvantages of the different types of trucks in their fleet. "The two of them were mortal enemies in that first budget meeting we had, but they've turned into quite a team," Anna said. "I think it's time to honor your promise to filter this down another level."

The supervisors went through all the same problems as the managers. For example, they low-balled the numbers to look good at first. But when they did, Bob told his managers to ask them why they were wrong. A bit embarrassed, the next time they tried to be more accurate. But then some fell short of forecast. But that was OK, too, because they could then be asked why. Writing their forecasts down in front of everyone turned out to be a key—it forced people to make a personal, visible commitment.

"What started to happen," Adam told his manager, "was I started to think about what made it difficult to make expectations. As I did that, I started to see some problems I never had before. Maybe it was that some employees were taking too long for lunch or that we didn't have adequate storage space or that it was taking too long to get stuff off the high shelves and we needed some other way to get it down faster. Little things, but they add up."

After another six months, in fact, the supervisors had gotten sufficiently charged up about the process they wanted to get employees involved beyond just telling them the numbers.

Adam got the OK to try it out in warehouse. He came up with the idea of having each group of employees actually write down a goal for their operation related to the specific measure of production relevant to them (order turn rate, for instance or returns on shipments). Each month they posted and reviewed the numbers then talked about the variances between actual and forecast. Employees came up with a lot of good (and not so good) ideas to address the problem.

Bob was pumped, and even Kevin now was becoming a convert. But Karen said they still hadn't closed the loop. "People now can contribute ideas on the numbers," she told Bob, "but just that. I think they've shown they actually have a lot of ideas—some that may go beyond just what they do or just how to improve their efficiency. Remember, Maggie told you there were several steps, and the last one was actual participation structures where people could meet to talk about ideas to make the business better. That's the last step we need to take."

"Karen, your team has earned a lot of goodwill with me. Let's do it," Bob said.

CHAPTER 9

Setting Up a System of Involvement

K aren recognized the first task was to set up an employee steering committee to help design and oversee the process. "I know you have some ideas on how to do this, Bob, including maybe even hiring someone to come set up something for us. But it is going to seem pretty strange to people to set up an employee involvement system and then tell the employees exactly how it will be run. I think we're better off with what may be a less perfect design but one that is ours."

By now Bob was excited enough about the progress that been made (and a little proud of himself for having moved it along) that he let Karen take charge.

Karen sent out an email to everyone on staff asking them to volunteer.

The response was, well, a thud.

Karen was not a happy camper. "Look," she told Jimmy, "I've really worked hard on this, and I ask for just a few volunteers and what do I get? People want to know if they do this will they get extra pay or why we should think Bob or Kevin are going to pay any more attention to this than they did to any of the ideas we suggested before with their famous open-door policy."

Jimmy hesitated for a minute and then said, "You know, to start, not even everyone has email, so they couldn't very well respond. And, anyway, some people heard about this and were not very happy about being seen as so second class. I think you need to be more careful to include everyone, and you actually might want to apologize to the folks who aren't on email. We need to have a meeting, and we need Bob and Kevin there, and they need to tell people they are really behind this, that they learned some lessons from what has happened in the last few years here and really want to make changes."

Bob and Kevin agreed, and they called an all-staff meeting the next week. "The open-door policy didn't work," Bob said. "I have to be honest about that. I was not very happy about that. I genuinely wanted your ideas and not much happened. So I thought you just didn't care that much. But I have learned that open-door policies almost never work. It's not enough. People need a structure, some specific way that you'll have opportunities to think about business issues and come up with ideas. The mini-games were a good start. But I want to get to the next level, where everyone here on a regular basis has some kind of way to share ideas and information.

"So what we need now is for you to help us figure out how to do that. Maybe it's meetings in each business area every couple of weeks, maybe it is teams to look at specific issues as they come up, maybe it's teams made up of people from across the company. I don't know. I want you to figure it out. I want you to own it."

Karen then outlined what was needed. "I need about seven people to volunteer for a committee to figure out how to get to whatever process we are going to use. And we're going to ask some people we really need to join anyway."

Fits and Starts...

Jimmy, Kim, Anna, and Thuy decided to volunteer. Three supervisors were added as well. Karen would be on the committee, too, and Bob could drop in from time to time, just to listen and provide support, not to make decisions. Bob would, however, have the ultimate say on whatever structure the committee suggested.

The committee started with a reading list (some of them are listed at the end of this book). They visited a couple of local ESOP companies with active employee involvement programs, went to a local meeting of ESOP companies focused on participation, sat in on an NCEO Webinar on the topic, and planned to send someone every year to the annual meeting.

They decided to keep the mini-games, to be used when and where needed as challenges came up. Then they added a simple structure with two parts:

1. *Area meetings:* Every two weeks, employees in each work area would meet for 30 minutes on work time. There would be a team leader selected by the group. The employees would have a chance to talk about problems and ideas. They were given a specific budget by Kevin (who needed a little coaxing from Bob to make it more than a token amount) and could use that for any work improvement they wanted. Any new ideas they agreed on, for now, would still be run by the manager most immediately responsible for that area. Bob told the managers to err on the side of letting people do what they want. Decisions were to be made by consensus; if consensus was not possible, then a vote was taken.

2. *Cross-functional teams:* Three cross-functional teams were set up: safety, work flow (a committee designed to look at how the different areas of the company worked together or to discuss problems or ideas that involved multiple areas), and customer satisfaction. The idea for the last group came from Anna, who'd read about companies where customers actually got to meet people doing the production, that sent line people to trade shows, and that even sent employees to visit customers sometimes. That way, people were doing something not just for their boss, but for Bob and Jennifer, whom they had met a few weeks ago. The committee would get the process going, then meet as needed to revise it.

The teams started off with a mixture of enthusiasm and trepidation, but some good ideas emerged, even if they later seemed like low-hanging fruit. The shipping department saved some time by buying new tape dispensers. Accounting found they could more aggressively negotiate with FedEx. HR started using Hotwire for hotel reservations for travelers whenever possible. The software people decided to build their own system instead of using the clunky off-the-shelf system their old boss liked. Warehouse decided to do a green audit and found they could actually sell some things they had thrown out for scrap recycling. The customer service team started having the people involved in getting a product or service off to a customer to include their business cards, with each person adding a personal signature.

It wasn't all sweetness and light. Esther's team in software spent weeks spinning its wheels. "We felt we needed to upgrade some of our equipment to be more productive, and we ran the numbers on it. But when we went to Rolf, he told us it wasn't in the budget and to forget it. Frankly we just about gave up after that."

Enrique said that they came up with a way to use more floor space for boxes now stored on top shelves, but the forklift drivers kept running into them. "It was really dumb," he said. "All they had to do was follow the new lines we painted, but they were so used to doing stuff the old way they just kept screwing up. People got pretty mad about that."

Some teams met and just griped. Others found that one or two negative people dominated the meeting; others found that a few excessively gung-ho types wouldn't let anyone else have a say. "There was this one guy, Richard, he just couldn't stop blabbing," Kim remembered. "The meetings were just a waste of time. He was a blowhard, and his work wasn't very good anyway. So we told our manager that it was him or us, and he got canned." Some managers just could not face giving up authority and either always said no or just kept putting decisions off. Some groups worked fairly well together but found they did not always have an issue to discuss. There were also more issues that needed coordination between groups because one group could not implement its ideas without help from another group.

Bob felt like he was working overtime helping other people try to solve problems that he could have solved better and faster on his own. When he complained to Karen, she said, "This is all new to these people. Just give us some time. We'll get better."

The steering committee had anticipated that getting "there" would not be easy. Rosario, ever the champion, saw these problems as opportunities. "No one expected us to hit a home run the first time up," she said. "So let's learn what is going wrong and see how we can fix it."

One new step was an inter-team coordination committee made up of one representative from each working team. It met for 30 minutes monthly but could meet more often if needed. A consultant was brought in to help train team leaders in running effective meetings, and all the team leaders could borrow the core books that the steering committee had found useful. Team leaders met every two months to trade ideas, a process Rosario hoped would not be necessary after a year or two.

Getting front-line supervisors trained in this new form of management was one of the toughest challenges. Bob knew from the other company leaders he had met that there could be some resistance to these new ideas because it may seem threatening to some people who may fear they are losing some authority. Getting an outside training group to come in was one option, but Bob decided to take a simpler approach by sending people to employee ownership conferences that had panels on the topic, having them read the key books on employee involvement the steering committee had identified, and then having them meet with Bob and members of the steering committee to talk about what they learned. If that was not enough, Bob made a commitment to the committee to hire an outside trainer.

After several more months, some groups were going great, others not so well. Kevin liked to chide Bob about the wasted time in all these meetings (and a lot of employees agreed), but as a numbers guy, he had to agree progress was being made. He added up all the costs of labor time "wasted" in the meetings, compared to it reduced cost generated by the new ideas and profitable business the ideas sometimes created, and saw the balance was clearly to keep the participation process going.

It would be a continuous improvement process, with steps back and forward. But more people were getting more done and having more fun doing it—even (maybe especially) Bob.

CHAPTER 10

Incentive Plans and Other Missteps

Now that the new system was moving forward, Bob thought it would be time to change the company's incentive plans. As things stood, there were bonuses for key managers based on individual performance appraisals. For everyone else, pay was mostly set by a formula, but individual managers could give out discretionary bonuses.

From what Karen had heard at the conferences, that system did not align very well with what BTA was now trying to do. "We are supposed to all be in this together," she told Bob. "But the way the incentive system works now, we kind of pit people against one another. Only some people get bonuses, and no one really knows just how a manager decides who gets what. Some people think it's mostly just politics. I think we need something more predictable that everyone can participate in."

Kevin liked the idea of measurable results being linked to rewards. He told Bob, "For years, I have wanted to set up a system where we set out specific numbers key managers had to meet. If they meet them, then they get a bonus; if not, they don't. Everyone knows just what they and we need to do.

"For everyone else, I really like Jack Welch's ideas. I think he is the best thing going right now in management advice. His idea is that the top 20% or so of the performers produce the most—maybe 80% of the improvement. So they're the ones who should get the biggest rewards. The bottom 20% or so shouldn't get anything, and maybe the lowest should get fired. Everyone in the middle can be eligible for small rewards. We'll come up with a specific way to rank people based on a series of metrics you and Karen and I can come up with."

Karen was not so sure. "Kevin, I see this 80-20 thing every time I pick up an HR magazine. But I wonder, is it just a myth? I never see any actual research to show this 'rule' really works. Anyway, I'd like to think that we can do better than just 20% of our people really contributing."

Bob wanted to believe Karen, but he felt he had done little but override Kevin throughout this whole process. He could see Kevin starting to get that faraway look on his face he sometimes got. He could see he was really steaming—and he would come to Bob later to talk about it. Not giving in on this might be the last straw for Kevin, and Bob did not want to lose him.

"I can see your point, Karen. But let's give Kevin a shot on this."

Over the next several weeks, the three of them worked to create a series of measures. For each group a key measure was picked. For warehouse, it was the number of packages damaged or returned. For sales, it was the number of new customers. For software, it was the number of programs shipped. Each employee was rated on his or her contribution to those goals by his or her supervisor. Eighty percent of the bonus available would go to the top 20% of the people, with the rest divided among the next 60%. Half of the bottom 20% was put on probation.

One year later, everyone agreed the system was a mess. Warehouse quality went up, but the number of packages shipped went down. The opposite happened in software, where more programs shipped but quality slipped. And more new customers were brought on line but not always at a profit.

Even worse, the system pitted people against one another. "Here we have these teams set up, but if I help out somebody else and spend time doing it, maybe he gets a better rating than I do," Enrique complained. Adam said that as a supervisor, he now had to worry about firing people all the time. In fact, he hired a couple of new people that year just so he could fire them at the end of the year, just to keep everyone else happy.

Rosario wasn't happy, either, and she was one of the winners. "People resented me. They said I was just good at office politics. People who were my friends now started being more distant. It was all so competitive; it just wasn't worth it. And people getting low bonuses started wondering if the company really valued them."

Even Kevin had to agree that the system failed, and the numbers showed it. He still thought they could be tweaked to make it better, but this time Bob put his foot down. It was indeed the last straw for Kevin. He handed in his two weeks' notice the next day.

Bob was sorely tempted to try to give in and get Kevin back. But Carol told him it was time to walk the walk. "This is going to be seen as a real test for you Bob. You can keep Kevin, but who are going to lose? And what credibility will you have on all this 'ownership culture' stuff you have been bragging about?"

Bob decided Carol was right. He went to the ESOP committee and asked members to come up with something better. At the very least it would be "owned" by the employees, so even if it were less perfect than in theory, it might work better in practice.

The committee created a new plan based on some ideas they had picked up at meetings. There would be two goals. The first would be overall profit, because ultimately that was really the bottom line. The second would be a year-to-year number picked by management and the committee based on some special goal that year, such as finding new customers. A bonus pool of 12% of profits was set up. Half that pool (6%) would be awarded for meeting the profit goal and half for meeting the customer goal. A "stretch" goal was also created that would create a 16% of profits pool. Everyone would get a share based on salary. After all, the committee reasoned, salary was a good measure of how much management thought people were contributing overall.

The committee guessed the system wouldn't be perfect and would need to be changed, but the process seemed much fairer.

Kevin, by the way, got a new job at an accounting firm. He could do his own work and not be responsible for managing anything. It sounded great.

Conclusion

Over the next few years, Bob came to see why Maggie had such a gleam in her eye talking about "ownership culture." BTA had a number of systems up and running. The regular and ad hoc teams were working so well that they were given increased autonomy to make and implement decisions on their own. The company was averaging two new ideas per employee. Many were small ideas that led to small improvements; a few were significant changes that led to new lines of business, much higher customer satisfaction, and greater efficiency. An employee team took over financial training. Numbers of various performance metrics were generated by the teams and posted every week. To be sure, a lot more time was spent meeting and learning, but the new ideas that came out of these efforts made it all more than worthwhile. It was also just a lot more fun to work there. More people felt engaged; managers could stop focusing so much on telling people what to do and focus instead on what they really liked to do and did well.

It wasn't magic, though. There were still cynics; there were still people who did just enough to get by. But the number had fallen, and most of these people would not end up sticking around.

For Bob, the payoffs were more than financial. In fact, Bob was now speaking at meetings and inviting participants in new ESOPs to come visit. He liked the fact that despite all the competition he not only did not have to lay any more people off but added more employees and was even thinking of doing an acquisition. He was so charged up about it that Carol had to warn him not to bore people at dinner parties with talk about business. What kept coming back to Bob was something Maggie had told him years before. "Bob," she told him, "I know that ESOPs can help make a business make more money. And I like money as well as anyone else. But I'll tell you what. I am 67 now, and I hope to live a good long time, but I do look back now and ask what made me proudest in my career. And it wasn't making money or even being the CEO. It's when Jimmy, who'd been a janitor for 20 years for us, came to me at my retirement party and said, 'Maggie, I worked all my life as a janitor, and most of it, no one cared what I thought or even thought I might actually have a good idea. At this company I was a real person. I felt like I mattered here. And I'll always be grateful for that.' When I think about my life, it's that janitor and a lot of other people who told me they felt the same way. That is what I want to be remembered for."

Just a few weeks earlier, Bob had had a similar experience. Enrique was leaving the company to help his son start a new small business. His ESOP stake could help them get it going. He was excited about the prospect but sad to leave. He told Bob that when his company hired people, BTA would be his model. "When I talk to friends, I talk about how great it is to work here, how you get to grow and use your mind and, well, how we all act like adults. They complain about their boss. I just hope you got something good out of this whole experience, too."

Ownership Culture Resources

NCEO Resources

Books

    The ESOP Committee Guide

    The ESOP Communications Sourcebook

Meetings

    Getting the Most Out of Your ESOP (every fall)

    Webinars on ownership culture

    NCEO annual conference (every spring)

Other Books

    Harvey Robbins and Michael Finley, *Why Teams Don't Work*

    Dean Schroeder, *Ideas Are Free*

    Jack Stack, *The Great Game of Business*

Other Meetings

    The Gathering of the Games (annual meeting of the Great Game of Business, each spring)

Suggested Exercises

Do You Know What People Really Think?

Getting to know what people really think about the ESOP can be tricky. One way to get an idea is to have employees sit in small groups and come up with a group statement of what they think *other people* think. Why other people? Because this way people will be more honest.

Once you know, ask these same groups to come up with some ideas to make things better. Each table can report back, and then an action list can be created.

The Plastics Engineering Problem

In this book, Plastics Engineering says it will no longer use BTA as a supplier unless it can cut prices significantly. Create a scenario like this that might actually happen in your company—something that might cause an important customer to leave.

Ask employees to form groups of eight or so people and come up with a process to figure out how to respond. Give each group 15 minutes, then have each group report what it decided to do.

Empty Open Doors

Does your company have an "open door" policy? Do people actually use it? If not, what's going on?

Here is a chance to do some role playing. Have one group of employees be the managers whose doors are supposedly open. Have group of a managers play employees who have ideas but can't seem to get a hearing. Ask the managers to tell the employees about the open-door policy and what they hope to accomplish. Have the employees tell the managers why they don't go in the door. Ask the managers to respond to that; then get a rebuttal from employees.

You can go back and forth on several obstacles (time, ideas that don't work, lack of feedback, etc.).

It is important to tell people to stay within their roles, not say what they actually think. When you are done, have the group come up with ways to make open-door policies more effective.

Getting Started on Employee Involvement

One approach to starting an employee involvement programs is— surprise—to get employees involved in its design. A simple way to get started is to ask employees to count off by six and divide into groups (you count off so that people can sit with people they didn't come in with and already know).

Ask everyone in the group to write down one thing that makes it hard for employees to share an idea or a problem that needs solving. Then write down an idea of how it might be made easier. Ask people to be very specific—not "we don't trust each other enough," or "we don't communicate well enough," but something like "the shifts never get a chance to meet," or "there is no easy place to submit a suggestion," or "when I make a suggestion, I don't get feedback." Ideas might be to create an ad-hoc team to address a particular problem or post suggestions on a bulletin board and show the answers.

Once they have written down their thoughts, spend 10 minutes at each table asking each employee to present them, one by one, with no discussion. Then spend five minutes discussing the ideas and coming up with the two best. Do this first for barriers and second for solutions.

Each group facilitator then reports back the two ideas. Have each table present just one idea and go around the room, then start again. You'll find a lot of overlap. Pick the top several ideas and assign an employee-management committee to come up with specific steps to put the ideas in place.

Sharing Numbers

There are a lot of good ways to get people involved in sharing financials. To get started, bring employees together and divide into groups based on their functions. Ask each group to spend 20 to 30 minutes coming up with what they think their critical number is and suggest a time frame to beat or meet it and a fun award if they win.

Another good idea is when the financials are presented, give everyone a blank income statement and have tables of employees guess the numbers. Then when the real data are presented, people will be primed to listen. You can give out awards for the best and worst guesses.

Open Space

Open space is a simple idea for getting employee feedback. Pick several critical issues, whether generic (improving safety) or specific (how to deal with a type of customer complaint). Then ask employees to go to the part of the room for people who want to talk about that issue. Give each group 15 to 20 minutes to come up with ideas and report back.

A Subject Guide to An Ownership Tale

Communication

    Problems typically faced in explaining ESOPs: Chapter 1
    Sharing bad news: Chapter 2
    Deciding how much information to share: Chapter 2
    Key principles of effective communication: Chapter 4
    Newsletters: Chapter 4

Employee participation systems

    Employee suggestion systems: Chapter 3
    Open-door policy: Chapter 3
    Problem solving teams: Chapter 5
    Team-based management: Chapter 9
    Where to start: Chapter 5

Incentive plans: Chapter 10

Sharing financial information

    Great Game of Business: Chapters 6 and 7
    Mini-Games: Chapter 8
    Open-book management: Chapters 6 and 7
    Sample income statement: Chapter 7
    Open-book management: Chapters 6 and 7

Suggested exercises: Appendix

About the Author

Corey Rosen is the NCEO's senior staff member and former executive director. He cofounded the NCEO in 1981 after working for five years as a professional staff member in the U.S. Senate, where he helped draft legislation on employee ownership plans. Before that, he taught political science at Ripon College. He is the author or coauthor of many books and over 100 articles on employee ownership, and coauthor (with John Case and Martin Staubus) of *Equity: Why Employee Ownership Is Good for Business* (Harvard Business School Press, 2005). He was the subject of an extensive interview in *Inc.* magazine in August 2000; has appeared frequently on CNN, PBS, NPR, and other network programs; and is regularly quoted in the *Wall Street Journal,* the *New York Times,* and other leading publications. He has a Ph.D. in political science from Cornell University.

About the NCEO

The National Center for Employee Ownership (NCEO) is widely considered to be the leading authority in employee ownership in the U.S. and the world. Established in 1981 as a nonprofit information and membership organization, it now has more than 3,000 members, including companies, professionals, unions, government officials, academics, and interested individuals. It is funded entirely through the work it does.

The NCEO's mission is to provide the most objective, reliable information possible about employee ownership at the most affordable price possible. As part of the NCEO's commitment to providing objective information, it does not lobby or provide ongoing consulting services. The NCEO publishes a variety of materials on employee ownership and participation, provides online education, and holds dozens of seminars, Webinars, and conferences on employee ownership annually. The NCEO's work includes extensive contacts with the media, both through articles written for trade and professional publications and through interviews with reporters. It has written or edited several books for outside publishers during the past two decades. The NCEO maintains an extensive Web site at www.nceo.org.

NCEO members receive (1) our bimonthly newsletter on employee ownership issues, (2) access to the members-only area of our Web site, (3) substantial discounts on publications, events, and services, (4) free live Webinars, and (5) the right to contact us for answers to questions. It costs $90 to join the NCEO for one year ($100 outside the U.S.). To join or order books, visit our Web site at www.nceo.org or telephone us at 510-208-1300.

Selected NCEO Publications

The NCEO offers a variety of publications on employee ownership and participation; below are a few of our main books. For more information, visit www.nceo.org or call us at 510-208-1300. Most of our books are also available in digital format.

Employee Stock Ownership Plans (ESOPs)

- *Understanding ESOPs* is an overview of the issues involved in establishing and operating an ESOP. It covers the basics of ESOP rules, valuation, and other matters, and then discusses hiring consultants and managing an ESOP company.

   $25 for NCEO members, $35 for nonmembers

- *Selling Your Business to an ESOP* focuses on the concerns of closely held businesses that are considering an ESOP sale, including the Section 1042 tax-deferred rollover.

   $25 for NCEO members, $35 for nonmembers

- *Leveraged ESOPs and Employee Buyouts* combines a discussion of legal, accounting, and valuation issues with an extensive discussion of leveraged ESOP financing.

   $25 for NCEO members, $35 for nonmembers

- *S Corporation ESOPs* introduces the reader to how ESOPs work and then discusses the legal, valuation, administrative, and other issues associated with S corporation ESOPs.

   $25 for NCEO members, $35 for nonmembers

- *The ESOP Committee Guide* describes the different types of ESOP committees, the goals they can address, alternative structures, member selection criteria, training, committee life cycle concerns, and more.

   $25 for NCEO members, $35 for nonmembers

- *ESOP Valuation* brings together and updates where needed the best articles on ESOP valuation that we have published.

  $25 for NCEO members, $35 for nonmembers

- *Don't Do That* is a guide to common mistakes in operating an ESOP and what to do about them.

  $25 for NCEO members, $35 for nonmembers

- *The ESOP Company Board Handbook* is a guide for board members in ESOP companies.

  $25 for NCEO members, $35 for nonmembers

- *Executive Compensation in ESOP Companies* discusses executive compensation issues, special ESOP considerations, and a survey of executive compensation in ESOP companies.

  $25 for NCEO members, $35 for nonmembers

Equity Compensation Plans

- *The Decision-Maker's Guide to Equity Compensation* explains how equity compensation plans work and what the considerations are for choosing and designing them.

  $25 for NCEO members, $35 for nonmembers

- *Equity Alternatives: Restricted Stock, Performance Awards, Phantom Stock, SARs, and More* is a complete guide, including model plans, to phantom stock, restricted stock, stock appreciation rights, performance awards, and more.

  $35 for NCEO members, $50 for nonmembers

- *Equity Compensation for Limited Liability Companies* describes how equity compensation works in an LLC and provides model plan documents.

  $25 for NCEO members, $35 for nonmembers

Ownership Culture

- This book, *An Ownership Tale,* is an easy-to-read short book, told in the form of a story about a fictional company, that draws on years of real-life experience about the challenges and solutions to creating an effective ownership culture.

  $5 for NCEO members, $10 for nonmembers